IT ALL BEGINS WITH SELF

How to Discover Your Passion, Connect with People, and Succeed in Life

By

Delano Lewis

Published by Best Seller Publishing®, Pasadena, CA
Best Seller Publishing® is a registered trademark
Printed in the United States of America.

ISBN-13: 978-1514196861
ISBN-10: 1514196867

This publication is designed to provide accurate and authoritative information with regard to the subject matter covered. It is sold with the understanding that the publisher is not engaged in rendering legal, accounting, or other professional advice. If legal advice or other expert assistance is required, the services of a competent professional should be sought. The opinions expressed by the authors in this book are not endorsed by Best Seller Publishing® and are the sole responsibility of the author rendering the opinion.

Most Best Seller Publishing® titles are available at special quantity discounts for bulk purchases for sales promotions, premiums, fundraising, and educational use. Special versions or book excerpts can also be created to fit specific needs.

For more information, please write:
Best Seller Publishing®
1346 Walnut Street, #205
Pasadena, CA 91106
or call 1(626) 765 9750
Toll Free: 1(844) 850-3500
Visit us online at: www.BestSellerPublishing.org

Table of Contents

Introduction

For some time, I have had a longing to share stories from my life in order to teach and motivate people for their walk through life. Over the years, I have been traveling across the country and sometimes around the world, giving speeches about how to succeed. With this book, I can share my experiences with a broader community.

It is also an opportunity for me to give my immediate family more details of my life so that they can understand my career and my life experiences. My immediate family includes my spouse, Gayle, who has been a strong partner in our marriage of 54 years, our 4 adult sons, and our 11 grandchildren.

My purpose for sharing these stories and life lessons is that I have a deep desire to show the readers how to connect with people, how to discover your passion, and how to succeed in life.

I was born in Arkansas City, Kansas, which is a town in southern Kansas, near the Oklahoma border. I grew up with two linguistic challenges. The first of which was that I was born in Arkansas City, Kansas, and after I had moved to Kansas City, Kansas, as a young child, many of my friends thought I was born in the state of Arkansas because the city is spelled the same way. However, it is pronounced (Ar-Kansas).

My second challenge was the fact that my name is Delano. Many would pronounce it incorrectly. They would pronounce it the same way as Franklin Roosevelt's middle name, Delano (Del-a-no). However, my name is pronounced (D-ley-no).

My parents moved to Kansas City, Kansas, when I was about 2 or 3 years of age. My mother was a high school graduate from Arkansas City High School. My father only had an 11th-grade education, and he worked as a manual laborer. He moved to Kansas City, Kansas, looking for better job opportunities. There he found a position as a day porter, or what they called a chair car attendant, with the Santa Fe Railroad. He kept this job for 37 years.

Looking back on my life, I see the value of a strong "family" unit or support system. A family unit could be, for example, a mother and father, an uncle, an aunt, a brother, a sister, or a good friend. In my case, my mother and father were my family unit and support system.

My father was very passive in many ways, but he did speak up during some very important times in my life. He was a hard worker, and he enjoyed his job. "Hard work will pay off," was his value system. He brought the paycheck home, and we lived very modestly, but relative to the time, I believe we did very well. My dad spent a lot of time away as a chair car attendant. He was usually home two days and gone two days. Since I was an only child, I spent a great deal of my time with my mother.

As a high school graduate, my mother was well read and forward-looking. She had a very strong influence on my value system, and she exposed me to many parts of the outside world. She enjoyed books, and she enjoyed music. Because of her interest in music, she encouraged me to learn to play an instrument. I started learning the violin, and later I went on to play the trumpet. My mother also encouraged me to dance, so I took tap dancing lessons from the time I was seven, and I continued taking them all the way through high school.

The community we lived in was segregated by race. We lived in a black neighborhood, and my school was all black until the '54 Supreme Court decision declared that segregation of white and Negro children in public schools only based on race was unconstitutional.

My mother would say to me, "There is a world out there that you need to know." She wanted to take me to a lunch counter in downtown Kansas City, Kansas, which was only a few blocks from our home. However, I did not particularly want to go because we had to eat in one specific section of the lunch counter. We could not eat with whites; we had to eat in what was called "The Colored Section." I was hesitant about doing that, but Mom said, "I want you to experience eating out, and I want you to feel comfortable as you enjoy a meal away from home." Spending that kind of time with me, and giving me a broader view of the world was one of her many assets.

High school was a very important part of my early background. I attended Sumner High School, named for

Charles Sumner. Charles Sumner was a Senator from the State of Massachusetts. On May 22, 1856, he was attacked and brutally beaten with a cane by a member of the House of Representatives, Preston Brooks. Sumner, who was an anti-slavery advocate, was attacked because he actively supported the admission of Kansas into the Union as a free state.

Sumner High School was an all-black school. It had extremely capable teachers. The teachers, too, were black, and they cared about their students. Because of their race, they could not find jobs other places, so they spent a great deal of time with us and gave us superb instruction.

Many of my teachers became role models to me. My science teacher, my chemistry teacher, my biology teacher, my band teacher, and my principal were all African-American men. Most of them had gone to the University of Kansas, which was only about 40 miles up the road from Kansas City, Kansas. Many of them pledged the predominantly black fraternity called Alpha Phi Alpha. These men were models of success that I emulated.

My high school principal, Mr. Solomon Thompson, had a particular influence on my life. Mr. Thompson was not only my principal, but he was also my neighbor. That had its blessings and its curses. He would see me when I would leave on a date, and he would be walking the dog when I returned home late at night. But he was also very supportive of me and my efforts during my high school years. I was a very diligent student. In addition, I was the drum major of the high school band and a part of the

National Honor Society. Mr. Thompson appointed me, along with my close friend, Dan Matthews, as delegates to Kansas Boys State in Wichita, Kansas.

Becoming a delegate was a turning point in my life. Boys State is an American Legion project, which continues to this day. Boys are chosen as delegates, between their junior years and senior years in high school. The mission of Boys State is to teach American government through active participation. The Boys Starters organize mock city, county, and state governments.

It was the first time that I interacted with students of other races. I competed with boys from all across the state of Kansas, who had been selected by their respective high schools and community groups.

Instead of being overwhelmed by this experience, I flourished. I ran for mayor of my small city at Boys State. I also ran for Supreme Court justice. I was elected mayor, and I was elected one of the seven Supreme Court Justices. In addition, I was the drum major of the Boys State Band. I had a tremendous experience and began to gain confidence that this young kid from a segregated school could compete with the best of them in the state of Kansas. My high school education at Sumner and my Boys State experience helped to increase my self-confidence.

Education and skills development are critical elements for success. Your goal should be to develop your skills in whatever areas that interest you. These interests could be anything from working with your hands, to science, to the performing arts.

There are many places you can go to develop your skills. If you have the opportunity to go to college, you can gain competence while you are there. Then you can build on that by going to graduate schools. You can study medicine, speech therapy, law, or one of the many other vocations.

You can also go to a community college and get a certification. Or you can take your general education and do internships in offices and businesses so that you learn how to do a job. Education in its broadest sense means developing your skills for productive work.

My support system, my neighborhood in Kansas City, Kansas, and my experiences in high school were key components of building my confidence. That is why I believe that a support network through a strong family unit, a caring neighborhood, and a strong educational foundation are paramount in your ability to succeed. All these elements play a role when you set out to discover your passion, connect with people, and succeed in life.

Chapter 1
Self-Discovery

It is paramount to your success to find out who you are. And in order to find out who you are, you need to do a self-assessment. What are your strengths and weaknesses? Assessing who you are is taking inventory of what you do well. Usually, people enjoy doing the things at which they are likely to succeed. But you also need to be aware of some of those things at which you are not quite as good. Once you know your strengths and weaknesses, you need to capitalize on your strengths.

I began my self-assessment in high school. The Supreme Court desegregated schools in 1954. So when I started Sumner High School in '53, it was still segregated. Like I mentioned in the previous chapter, the teachers at Sumner cared for their students, and I thrived there. I excelled in music, theater, and dance. I was the drum major of the high school band, and I was also a part of the National Honor Society and International Club. These experiences led me to understand what things I did well. In my assessment, public speaking came naturally to me. I wondered if there was some way I could turn that talent into a profession.

I was also a young leader in Eighth Street Baptist Church in Kansas City, Kansas. The pastor of the church, Reverend I.H. Henderson, Sr., was a very dynamic minister who was active in community affairs, civil rights, and the NAACP local chapter in Kansas City, Kansas. I admired his speaking style, and I used to imitate it. He would read aloud a passage from the Bible, and then he would apply it to everyday life and give the parishioners a message on how they could adjust in society. The reverend was a role model for me. I listened carefully to his sermons and how he delivered the message, and I began to emulate his style and approach.

My mother was always interested in helping our neighbors and worked as a volunteer in the community. Whether it was for a neighbor or a girl or boy in the community who might need some extra clothes, she was always sewing. She always served others. Her example instilled in me a sense of caring for others. Because of this upbringing, I did not only want to find something that I could do and do well, but I also wanted to serve and help people.

I saw that I was capable of speaking, inspiring, and leading, and I began to contemplate how I could use those capabilities for a productive career.

I originally thought about speech therapy as a way of putting my speaking skill to good use. I considered going to school so that I could learn how to help people who have difficulties with speech overcome those difficulties. That would be an opportunity for me not only to make my skill productive, but also to help people.

Eventually, I moved away from the idea of speech therapy, and I began considering the law. As a lawyer, I could become a prosecutor or judge, but I did not particularly gravitate in that direction because I had a mindset of serving others.

Growing up in the 50s in a segregated community, where lunch counters, schools, and public accommodations were segregated by race, also had an impact on me. I felt that the Civil Rights marches were important, and I always believed in non-violence. I also felt that the rule of law and its application in society was important.

There were laws that denied blacks the right to certain public accommodations, laws that denied blacks the right to vote and laws that denied blacks the right to apply for certain jobs. People made all those rules and regulations.

I believed that people could change those rules, regulations, and laws. That was when I said to myself that I could use the law to serve and change society. I thought that with a career in the law, I could help those who were less fortunate in society. In particular, I could help other minorities who were fighting against racial discrimination and prejudice.

My Sumner High School yearbook in 1956 listed all of the activities in which I had participated. It also listed my ambition as wanting to be a lawyer.

After I had graduated from high school, I went to college at the University of Kansas and graduated in 1960. In 1963, I graduated from Washburn University School of Law, passed the Kansas Bar, and became a lawyer in Kansas.

I had begun taking inventory very early. In high school, I had role models who led me toward developing my skills, and I could see that my talents were in speaking and leading, so I began to pursue my career in the law.

When you are in school, you are presented with a range of subjects. Perhaps you find that you excel in the science subjects, for example, mathematics, chemistry, and biology. Or you might find that you do well in physical education. Then you can capitalize on your athletic ability. Or perhaps you have a good understanding of the social sciences such as history and government, psychology, and sociology.

After you have taken inventory of your strengths, you should try to determine how you could apply those strengths to productive work. In our society, being productive leads to self-esteem and self-confidence.

You might find that you need help developing those strengths or that you need more skills training and education in order to make those strengths work for you. If so, then that is something you should do.

My advice is to do a self-assessment and to look for the strengths on which you can capitalize. Then ask yourself: Is there a way I can take those strengths and apply them to productive work? By doing so, you are taking the first steps to achieving a successful life.

Chapter 2
Education as the Foundation for Success

Education was talked about over and over in my family. It was preached that in order to succeed, you need that strong foundation. My neighbors and friends in Kansas City, Kansas, said that in order to be productive in society, get the job you are interested in, and support your family, you need strong skills and a strong educational foundation.

Education and skill development is the way out of poverty in our society. Many of my friends growing up who did not go to college went off to the military. In the military, they learned skills such as mechanical engineering, which prepared them to work with trucks, planes, and automobiles.

A family friend of ours, Elmer Bass, was a construction worker. He would come to our house and talk about his skills as a construction worker. He learned his profession through a federal program, the Civilian Conservation Corps, established by President Franklin Delano Roosevelt. In this program, men and women learned how to use their hands for productive work.

The importance of education was emphasized at my school. Many of the teachers there had experienced discrimination. They wanted to train us so that we perhaps could avoid some of their mistakes and take advantage of opportunities when those opportunities came. My role models at Sumner High School set the stage for me for the future. My chemistry teacher, my science teacher, my band teacher, and my principal were all strong African-American men who were great examples. Many of these teachers had attended the University of Kansas, which was why I in turn chose to study there.

My mother and father advised me to go to college, and they promised to make every effort to see to it that I had the funds and the wherewithal to do that.

In 1956, I graduated from Sumner and went on to the University of Kansas. Within a semester, I had pledged Alpha Phi Alpha fraternity and soon became an Alpha fraternity brother on the campus at KU.

In Alpha Phi Alpha, I learned more about how to succeed and how to use the courses that I was taking to enhance my career. I still had a passion for helping people, so I took a pre-law program in political science and history. In most law schools, you need an undergraduate degree to be admitted to law school. Many of us went the political science, government, and history route because most of our American laws are based on English common law. A study of English history will give you a leg up in understanding our legal system in America.

After I graduated in 1960, I went on to Washburn School of Law in Topeka, Kansas. I was fulfilling my dream of using my speaking talents. My vision was to use the law to pursue a career in an area of civil rights. I believed that applying the law in a progressive direction would help change society.

By doing a self-assessment, you will hopefully discover your niche. The next step is finding the proper forum that will help you enhance your skills.

Today, information is prolific. You can gather so much information from the Internet and other sources that there is very little excuse for people not to find the answers to their questions.

In my day, it was more difficult to gather information about where to enhance your skills. You could get it by word of mouth, from your teacher, from your principal, or from your church.

Finding a place where you can develop your skills is a part of your self-discovery process. You will need to consider where you can go and what you can afford. What is realistic?

If you have an interest in food, nutrition, and food service, you could go to a community college that provides certificates in culinary arts and get a certification. With the certification, you might be able to find a job as a chef or something else in the food service industry.

If mechanics is your field of interest, you could do the same in that field and become a mechanical engineer or an electrician.

The military is another option. By joining the military, you would not only help protect and serve our country, but you could also get into a skills program that would help you enhance your ability to be productive.

A part of self-discovery and self-assessment is finding your strengths and determining how to develop and enhance them. Always keep in mind that whether you are pursuing a job or starting your own business, certain skills are needed to succeed.

In my case, my high school teachers and neighbors helped me find my path. Several of my neighbors went to the University of Kansas, so that was a natural choice for me. I had even gone to a summer camp there, and it was only 40 miles from home. It was an affordable option, and I was comfortable with it. Deciding to go to the University of Kansas was one result of my self-discovery, and it was a very important part of my life.

Whether the education comes from basic skill training, a college or a university, it is the key to your development. It is critical to achieving success. It is critical to your survival. It is even critical to happiness.

I am strongly convinced that productivity in our society is related to self-esteem and self-confidence. Our jails and prisons are inhabited by a vast majority of African-American men and Hispanic men. My guess is that over two-thirds of our prisons are full of minority men who have low self-esteem and low level of confidence because they have, for different reasons, failed to be productive. They do not have skills that would allow them to make a contribution to society. It is a downward spiral.

There is, however, also an upward spiral you can choose. By developing your skills, you can be productive. Productivity leads to self-esteem, and self-esteem leads to self-confidence. Small successes also lead to greater self-esteem and self-confidence.

I believe that education in its broadest sense is critical for your psychological wellbeing. In my case, it provided the roadmap for my career. It gave me the chance to expand my horizons, which had been limited in my black segregated community in Kansas City, Kansas.

You do not have to go to college in order to learn something new. You can go to your local library to expand your horizons.

I had that opportunity to expand my horizons, and I implore others to take advantage of their opportunity to expand theirs because it can create an upward spiral that leads to a better life.

Chapter 3
Believe in Yourself

Belief in yourself is related to your self-discovery, self-assessment, self-confidence, and self-esteem. You should have a lot of one-on-one time with yourself so that you can understand your own personality and capabilities.

You need to understand what things you do well and also what things frustrate you, and you do not do well. It all comes back to your self-confidence and your belief in yourself.

We can make excuses about life such as "I did not get that job because the boss did not like me," or "The interviewer did not like me." Or you may think, "I did not get that promotion because I am a woman," or "I did not get that promotion because I am a minority."

All of the above may be true, but you do not want to make those excuses if you lack the ability to do things. Your abilities come from hard work, studying, and your belief that you too can achieve. Yes, there is discrimination. Yes, there is prejudice. Yes, there are obstacles in the greater society, but you still need to believe that you can achieve what you set out to do and prepare yourself to excel at it.

Look at what you have already done. You can say to yourself, "I have succeeded on a math test." "I have done well on a geography test." "I ran the four-minute mile." "I did the marathon." "I cooked the greatest dessert." Tell yourself about your accomplishments. It will build your confidence, and believing in yourself leads to success.

My successes began early on with having the confidence to achieve. It began with my parents. My mother was strong and perhaps sometimes overprotective, but she believed in me. My father was somewhat passive, but when he did speak, his voice made a difference in the decision. He said, "Yes, you can achieve," and he promised that he and my mother would help me do the things that I wanted to do. No one told me I could not do all the things that I did. In particular my parents had confidence in me, and I began to have confidence in myself.

In 1958, while I was studying at the University of Kansas, I got to know a fellow student by the name of Gayle Jones. I invited her to be my date at a dance, and eventually we became a strong couple. I proposed to her on Thanksgiving of 1959, and in 1960, after we both graduated from college, we were married.

Gayle and I had one child during my first year of law school, and we had another child during the third year. At the same time, I worked 40 hours a week at the Children's Hospital of the Menninger Foundation. It is a hospital for the mentally ill. I worked with disturbed boys at the hospital. I also went to law school full time. I believed that I could do it. I wanted to fulfill my responsibilities as a spouse and parent. I wanted to support my young family. At the same time, I was developing the skills I needed to pursue my passion for becoming a lawyer.

When I first mentioned law school to my father many months prior to my engagement to Gayle, he said that he would help pay for it. After I had told him that I wanted to get married, he wondered about my plans for my education. I told him that law school was still my plan and that I would get a job and work while studying. I also explained that if we did not have kids right away, Gayle would work as well. He thought for a moment, and then he said, "I said I was going to help you through law school and I will." And so my parents helped me financially during law school even after I got married and started having a family.

In 1963, I graduated from law school. I had a strong belief in myself. However, I was not sure that a job would come my way. There was always the option of going into the private practice of law.

I decided that one possible way to support my family after graduating was to join the military. If I could join the Judge Advocate Corps and become a lawyer in the military, I could support my family while getting experience practicing law in the Air Force Judge Advocate program.

Washburn School of Law in Topeka, Kansas, was near Forbes Air Force Base. I took a physical examination for the Air Force hoping to be appointed to the Judge Advocate program.

Much to my disappointment, the doctor found a heart murmur. I was shocked. I talked to my mom about it because I had not known that I had any difficulties. She said that I had had asthma as a baby, and she thought it could be an outgrowth of the asthma. The heart murmur was enough to keep me out of the Judge Advocate Corps. That was a very big disappointment.

What do you do when you are faced with big disappointments? You persevere. You look at other options. Success in life comes from learning how to deal with Plan B when Plan A does not work. My Plan A of going to the Air Force did not work, so I had to think about Plan B.

My Plan B was to apply for the Honors Program at the Department of Justice. I applied and was appointed, so my first job after graduating law school was in Washington, D.C., in the Department of Justice.

When I went to the Justice Department in 1963, John F. Kennedy was President of the United States, and his brother Robert Kennedy was the Attorney General. I was one of only ten blacks in the Department of Justice. It was a very exciting experience because it was my first job as an attorney. I was pursuing my passion of the law, and it was well paid.

Shortly after, in 1965, I left the Justice Department and went to the Equal Employment Opportunity Commission when it first started. This was a continuation of my passion for working in civil rights.

Title VII of the Civil Rights Bill of 1964 dealt with employment discrimination. The Equal Employment Opportunity Commission was established in 1965, one year from the passage of the Civil Rights Bill. I began as a lawyer in 1965 with the Equal Employment Opportunity Commission.

My career began in the federal government. It began because I wanted to pursue my passion. Through my self-discovery process, I found that my desire was to use the law to help. I pursued my desire by going to law school and enhancing the necessary skills. I worked hard to get my law degree. Then I persevered to find my first job, and that first job led to my second job in the federal government.

After discovering who you are, believing in yourself is the key. You need to believe that you too can achieve what you desire.

Not everybody has a defined support system around him or her. Even though your family unit may be separated, or you may not have the support systems that I had when I grew up, there are other support systems available.

Believing in yourself and having confidence in yourself leads to openness to mentoring and openness toward those who want to support you. You have to be open to it. You have to be open to listening and responding.

Your support system could be a family member, your pastor, a person from the neighborhood, or a relative. The support systems are there; you just have to be open to them.

Once you are, they will help you build your confidence and ability to achieve that which you set out to do.

Chapter 4
The Value of Relationships

Relationships have been very important in my life and my career. The value of friendships and relationships is incredible. It is not just about networking. It is not only about trying to get from Point A to Point B or finding out whom you know who can help, but it is also about true relationships.

Opportunities will come if you listen and are open to mentors and support systems. If someone gives you advice or support, it is up to you to take it in. You need to listen to it and analyze what it means. And if it fits, take advantage of that opportunity. Try to be adventuresome. Consider taking some risks. These approaches can lead to great dividends and opportunities.

One of the relationships that had the greatest impact on my early career was the one with my next-door neighbor and her husband, Sue and David Coe. When I went to Washburn School of Law in Topeka, Kansas, Gayle and I lived in married student housing on the campus, and there Sue and Dave were our next-door neighbors.

Sue worked as a legal secretary for the United States Attorney's Office in Topeka. She was helping her husband, Dave, through his undergraduate education. Dave was planning to go to medical school at the University of

Kansas. After he finished his undergraduate education at Washburn, he was accepted to KU Medical School.

When they moved to Kansas City, Kansas, Sue transferred to the United States Attorney's Office there. She became the chief administrative assistant to the United States Attorney at that time, Newell George.

Mr. George had been a Congressman from Kansas City, Kansas, and he lost his bid for reelection in 1960. President John F. Kennedy was a good friend of Mr. George and named him United States Attorney for the State of Kansas after his loss for reelection.

Sue told me that there was an honors program for lawyers at the Department of Justice. She thought it was an excellent opportunity for me. We communicated, and I told her that I appreciated the thought, but I was working full time while going to law school full time, and my grades were okay, but I was not an honor student. She still encouraged me to apply.

I took Sue's advice and applied, and I had a fantastic interview with Mr. George. After the interview, he showed me around his office. There were pictures of the Kennedy family, including a picture of Robert Kennedy and a picture of President Kennedy in a hat, which you do not see too often. It was quite impressive to me as a young law student.

Within the next year – my last year of law school – I got word from Sue that Mr. George had sent a letter to Bobby

Kennedy. The letter said something along the following lines:

> Dear Bobby, I want you to meet this young man. He would have been an honor student if he had not worked 40 hours a week and supported his family. I was very impressed with him, and I would like to recommend him for the Honors Program at the Department of Justice.

Shortly after, I received a call informing me that I had been accepted to the Honors Program. That was my first job after law school, which I started in November 1963.

In other words, it was the opportunity that my next-door neighbor presented to me, and my grasping that opportunity that led to my first job out of law school.

The second relationship that played a significant part in the development of my career came with the creation of the Equal Employment Opportunity Commission.

Under Title VII of the Civil Rights Act of 1964, which was passed by Congress on July 2, 1964, the Equal Employment Opportunity Commission was established. Its mission was to eliminate employment discrimination based on race, color, sex, religion, or national origin. Due to an amendment introduced by Senator Everett Dirksen of Illinois and passed by the United States Senate, implementation of Title VII of the Civil Rights Act of 1964 was delayed for one year. It became effective on July 2, 1965.

America had waited for more than 200 years for equal employment opportunities for all. The country had also been waiting for elimination of discrimination in the workplace to be resolved. As a result of compromise in the Senate through the Dirksen Amendment, Title VII was delayed for a full year, to allow businesses time to get ready. Consequently, Title VII did not come into effect until July 1965.

A five-member commission was created under Title VII. The majority party, the Democrats, had three seats, and the minority party, the Republicans, had two seats. President Johnson nominated all five persons.

One of the Republican nominees was a close friend and a fellow Washburn Law graduate, Samuel C. Jackson. Sam was an active lawyer with the NAACP Legal Defense Fund. His law firm, Scott, Scott, Scott, and Jackson, was one of the firms that argued the Brown v. Board of Education of Topeka. It was the 1954 Supreme Court desegregation case, one of the five cases before the Supreme Court that led to the desegregation of public schools in America. Sam was nominated for one of the two Republican slots on the Equal Employment Opportunity Commission.

I gave Sam a call, and he was very receptive to it. In fact, he said he had been waiting for me to call him. We had known each other for some time, and he said, "You heard about my appointment. You have been in Washington for a couple of years. You know your way around, and you want to know how I can help you." Sam was quite prescient, and he understood why I made the call.

Again, I seized the opportunity that a close relationship afforded me. This time it was my relationship with a fellow Washburn Law graduate and a very talented lawyer. Through Sam Jackson, I became a part of a task force from the Department of Justice, which was made up of three lawyers. We were detailed from the Justice Department to the Equal Employment Opportunity Commission to help the EEOC set up its operations.

Shortly after I became a part of the task force, I managed to find a position in the Office of Compliance at the EEOC, and that was my second job in a good and successful federal career.

Chapter 5
Think and Build for the Long Term

Thinking and building long term require that you assess where you are in your career and where you would like to be. If you are forward-looking and have a sense of the bigger picture, and understand the vast possibilities ahead, the following ideas might help you think about next steps.

An adventuresome spirit, forward-looking ideas, and willingness to take risks are all imperative in order to experience new horizons. The key is to think about the big picture. Think about where you are, where you would like to be, and what the steps are to get there.

I have always had a passion for the law, and I felt that my strength of speaking and being able to influence people would be a perfect fit for the law. It was not my desire to become a judge or a prosecutor. Instead I wanted to use the law to make a positive impact on society. I wanted to serve with the law as a skill base. Therefore, I was very fortunate to have the positions I had at the Justice Department and the Equal Employment Opportunity Commission.

Then another opportunity presented itself, and it certainly made me think about the long term.

When I worked as an attorney in the Internal Security Division of the Justice Department, I became good friends with Roger Bernique. Roger was a Senior Attorney, and he was always interested in the up-and-coming new lawyers in the department.

My wife, Gayle, and I were invited to a dinner party at Roger's home one evening. At the party, we met a number of fascinating people. After an excellent meal and several glasses of wine, a woman by the name of Cynthia Courtney, who sat directly across from me at the table, leaned over to me and said,

"Delano, I'm just curious; would you ever consider moving to Africa?"

"Africa?" I asked. "I'm fresh out of Kansas. How could I go to Africa?"

"With the United States Peace Corps," she replied.

I said to her "I thought the Peace Corps was for young and unmarried people who volunteered their service."

Cynthia, very calmly, put my concerns at ease and said that if I were interested, I could go as part of the Peace Corps staff. She went on to say that being employed as Peace Corps staff would be a paid position and that I would be an employee of the federal government. I would also be able to bring my family, and the Peace Corps would provide housing for my family. At that moment, I was speechless while Gayle was thinking about all of the possibilities.

At the time, I was a lawyer and had had two very important jobs, one in the Justice Department and the other at the EEOC. Going into the Peace Corps and living and working in Africa were outside my comfort zone. I knew very well that if I were to take this job offer, I would move from using the law in my job to becoming more of an administrator. That was a choice I had to make.

You may have to make some choices along the way as well. As you consider how you can be productive, how you can succeed, and how you can take advantage of opportunities, you have to make decisions based on what fits you.

After some long conversations with my wife and other family members, I decided that I would take advantage of the opportunity that had presented itself and take the risk of working overseas for the Peace Corps. But I knew full well that it could mean moving further and further from the law.

In early 1966, I interviewed with Cynthia at the United States Peace Corps. I became fascinated with the work of the organization.

One of the first Peace Corps programs was in Ghana, West Africa. The Peace Corps had a great mission: to train people as teachers, community development workers, and, in some areas, health workers. They were often trained for only 30 days before they would go out and help in countries where they were invited to serve.

Cynthia was the desk officer for West Africa. We initially talked about a position in Sierra Leone, West Africa. However, the position that I was appointed to and accepted was Associate Peace Corps Director in Benin City, Nigeria.

Six months after I met Cynthia, Gayle and I, along with our three boys, ages 5, 3, and 2, took Pan American flight number 150 to Lagos, Nigeria, on our way to Benin City, Nigeria.

My job in the Peace Corps was to support about 200 volunteers in Midwest Nigeria. I worked with the Ministry of Education to make sure that the Peace Corps Volunteers were assigned to meaningful positions. I visited volunteer sites to see to it that they had the needed materials and supplies. As staff members, we were also counselors to the volunteers to assure their wellbeing and assist in their adjustment to the culture.

The position I held was administrative. I did not use my legal background, but I could use the organizational skills and discipline of the mind that I had learned in law school.

Peace Corps Nigeria was one of the largest programs with more than 800 volunteers in the country. It was a fascinating position. I had a chance to learn about working and living in another culture.

There was certainly some culture shock when we stepped off the plane to the warm, humid air in Lagos, Nigeria, in the summer of 1966. As we went to the Peace

Corps Director's home in Lagos, we saw people on the side of the road carrying things on their heads, bicycles and cars honking, and cattle running around. It was indeed different from life in America.

We were to live in the Midwest, which was the less developed part of Nigeria. We had a wonderful home, but only a few paved roads surrounded us, and there was a single small airport with planes that came in only once or twice a week.

With the 200 volunteers we had, we were making a difference in the country. However, after one year there, we had to evacuate because of the Nigerian Civil War.

Again, my career began to move. It seemed that the Peace Corps felt I had a great deal to offer, so after our year in Nigeria, they appointed me Country Director in 1967, in the East African country of Uganda. At age 28, I was in charge of 160 volunteers in the country of Uganda. All of these volunteers were teachers in elementary and secondary schools.

We lived in Kampala, which was a very different city from Benin. There were a few more paved roads, and the climate was very different. Nigeria had a tropical climate with a rainy season. Kampala, on the other hand, had a 78-degree temperature most of the time, and there were beautiful hills, gorgeous sugar plantations, and tea plantations. The people here were much more reserved than the Nigerians. They were very friendly and reserved, but the Nigerians were gregarious and friendly.

I worked closely with the government, and I became even closer to the U.S. mission because the U.S. Ambassador wanted me to be at his country team meetings once a week.

The marvelous experience of living and working overseas for three years happened because I was open and listened to the opportunity that was presented to me.

It was an exciting opportunity for the whole family. My wife and I went to Nigeria with our three children, and our fourth child was born in Uganda. Though I was moving away from the law, I gained a great deal in learning how to administer, how to run an office, how to relate to a government, and how to absorb another culture.

The key to all these great events was that I was forward-looking, trying to advance my career, and acting on my passions. If you want to experience new horizons, I advise you to do the same.

Chapter 6
Adapt to Change:
Move Out of Your Comfort Zone

As you reflect on your strengths, weaknesses, and the assessment of your personality and background, you should take a thorough look at your career.

One way to enhance your career is to move outside your comfort zone. Perhaps we enjoy the familiarity of where we are, but sometimes we need to think about trying something different. We need to consider new horizons. You might be afraid to go outside your comfort zone. However, such moves can enhance and expand your career.

On the one hand, going outside your comfort zone might stretch you, and that can be a little uncomfortable and frightening. On the other hand, it can be exhilarating and might add new dimensions to your life.

In 1969, my family and I returned to the U.S. By then I had served for three years in the United States Peace Corps in Nigeria and Uganda. Now I faced the challenge of picking up my career in a country that had undergone change since the last time I lived there.

1968 was a dramatic year in the U.S. Dr. Martin Luther King Jr. was assassinated in April that year. Shortly after,

Senator Robert Kennedy, who was making a run for the presidency of the United States, was assassinated.

After the assassination of Dr. King, there was a lot of anger, particularly in the black communities around the country, and riots erupted. This anger manifested itself in what was later called the Black Power Movement in the United States. The non-violent movement was still active, but since the assassination of Dr. King, many groups espoused a more militant behavior, and that gave rise to this movement. It consisted of African-Americans and some whites who believed that they could use any means necessary to achieve equal rights.

All of this was happening while we were living in Kampala, Uganda. When our tour ended in 1969, and we returned to America, more specifically the Washington, D.C., area, the country had changed.

I had been in some culture shock while serving in the Peace Corps in Nigeria and Uganda. Now, upon our return to the U.S., I had yet another culture shock because of the changes that had occurred while we had been abroad.

If you want to be successful and move your career and your life forward, you will have to adapt to change.

In this case, I had to adjust to a changed America. The assassinations of Dr. Martin Luther King Jr. and Senator Robert Kennedy impacted our country tremendously. They both believed strongly in equal rights and opportunities for all. For them to be taken from this world was quite distressing to many of us.

Upon our return to America, we had to be open to the changes and be willing to adapt to them. How was I to enhance my skills after spending several years living and working overseas? How was I to adjust back to life in the United States?

I came back from Africa as the Director of the East and Southern Africa Division of the Peace Corps. My job was to be an administrator in the organization's headquarters in Washington, D.C. My position was to oversee the Peace Corps staff and the programs in East and Southern Africa. In addition, I was recruiting minorities into the Peace Corps.

After having spent time as an administrator and living and working overseas, I asked myself what to do next. How was I to adjust to the changing American society?

Since Washington, D.C., is a political city made up of lawyers working inside and outside the government, it was a good fit for me as a lawyer and one interested in government.

I thought that it made sense for me to aim for a federal career. That was a career upon which I could build. I had started in the Justice Department, and I had gone on to the Equal Employment Opportunity Commission. From there I had gone to the Peace Corps, which is also a federal agency. Now I was keeping my eyes and ears open for other opportunities in the federal government.

I started looking and thinking, and I was open to change. I was very comfortable working in the executive branch of government. From my previous experience, I had learned how to use my legal training. I also had gained the skills of an administrator and manager, which I could use working in the executive branch of the government.

Although I was primarily looking to continue working in the federal government, I was open to considering changes in my career given the many changes that were occurring in America.

A good friend of mine from the Peace Corps, Roberta Lovingood, talked to me about expanding my horizons. Roberta worked with Peace Corps in Washington. She had a good friend in the office of Senator Edward Brooke of Massachusetts, who was on his first term at the time, in 1969.

Roberta's good friend in Senator Brooke's office was Rochelle Fashaw. Rochelle wanted to encourage Senator Brooke to bring an African-American into his Washington, D.C., office in a professional capacity.

Senator Brooke was the first African-American elected to the United States Senate since Reconstruction. He was in office from January 1967 to January 1979, and he was the only black in the United States Senate at that time. He had been Attorney General of the State of Massachusetts. When

Senator Leverett Saltonstall retired, Brooke ran for that vacated Senate seat and was elected.

Rochelle Fashaw felt that a professional African-American should be a part of Senator Brooke's office. She was African-American, but she was a caseworker in the office, and she thought that a lawyer, doctor, or engineer – someone of a professional status should work in his office as well.

Roberta referred my name to Rochelle. We met, and through her I learned of the possibility of a position as a legislative assistant. She talked to me about my background in the law and work overseas, and she wondered if I might have an interest in working in the office of Senator Brooke.

Once again, I faced moving out of my comfort zone; I chose to be open to moving from the executive branch of government to the legislative branch. I decided to apply for the position as legislative assistant, and my first interview was with the chief of staff, Alton Frye. It was a good interview. He told me, however, that they did not have the funds to hire me at that moment.

Time went by, and I remained open to changing careers while I was doing recruiting for the Peace Corps as well as my administrative job.

One day, as I was out in Minnesota recruiting, I received a call. It came from my wife who said that Senator Brooke had tried to reach me on the home phone number. I returned Brooke's call, and he communicated via his staff that he would like to interview me back in Washington.

I returned from my recruiting travels, and as I had never been to the state of Massachusetts and had no clue as to the state and politics, I prepared for my interview by doing some research.

The meeting with Senator Brooke went very well. I was impressed with him, and I like to think that he was impressed with me and my work history. As we concluded the interview, we talked about my coming on as a legislative assistant. I would be working on social legislation and all the legislation dealing with welfare, social security, education, and social issues. I accepted the offer, and I was delighted that I would be working for Senator Edward Brooke of Massachusetts. Keep in mind that in 1970 and 1971, there were very few black legislative assistants on Capitol Hill.

In this new job, I could use my background in the law and my past work experience, even though I was working in an area that was new to me – the legislative side of government. It was a very good job, and I enjoyed working with Senator Brooke. I quickly got up to speed on the politics of Massachusetts. My job was to alert the Senator to issues in the social arena and help him filter through these issues to determine if legislation should be needed.

After spending a year and a half in Senator Brooke's office, I was able to use my law degree in crafting legislation for the Senator.

As I was learning how the Senate works, there was an important election in Washington, D.C.

As background to that election, in 1800 our national government moved from Philadelphia to Washington, D.C., where our legislators carved out some land from Maryland and some land from Virginia and created the District of Columbia, which became the Federal District. Our forefathers envisioned that the primary purpose of the Federal District would be to provide a place for the seat of the presidency, the seat of Congress and the seat of the Supreme Court and other federal agencies.

Our forefathers did not think of the District of Columbia as a place where families would live. They did not foresee that people would be born and grow up in Washington, D.C. They thought that legislators would come and go keeping their voting residences in their home states. As a result, the citizens who were born in the District of Columbia, as well as those who were living there but had no voting residency outside the District, were disenfranchised.

In 1970, Congress made an effort to remedy this situation by creating the authority of citizens of the District of Columbia, to elect a non-voting delegate to represent them in the House of Representatives. That was a historic election for the citizens of the District of Columbia in 1970.

The person who was elected as a non-voting delegate from the District of Columbia to the House of Representatives was Walter Fauntroy, who was seated on

January 3, 1971. As a Baptist minister and confidant to Dr. Martin Luther King Jr., Fauntroy held the highest political office in the District of Columbia at that time.

As Fauntroy assembled his office staff, he looked to fill the position of chief of staff with an African-American. He was looking for an African-American who would push hard for social legislation. I heard about this opportunity through the legislative grapevine. I applied for the position because I thought this was another chance to enhance my federal career. I was a legislative assistant, but going to the House side as chief of staff was entirely different. It was another move out of my comfort zone.

As a part of the hiring process, Walter Fauntroy wanted me to interview with three of his close advisors. I met with Marion Barry, who was running Pride, Incorporated, a community organization in Washington, D.C. I also met with John Hechinger, a businessman who was one of Walter Fauntroy's top supporters. The third interview was with Jim Gibson of the Urban Institute, a community organization in Washington, D.C. I passed all three interviews with flying colors and was hired by Walter Fauntroy as his chief of staff.

Adapting to change and moving out of your comfort zone are critical to your success.

Upon my return to the United States, I thought that it made sense to build on my federal career, my experiences in the Justice Department, the Equal Employment

Opportunity Commission, the Peace Corps in Africa, and the Peace Corps in Washington, D.C.

However, when we came back to the U.S., the environment had changed, so I needed to adapt. I was open to looking at other federal government opportunities. Through a close friend, I was able to learn about the position on Capitol Hill. That opened up the world of the legislative branch of government.

Between 1969 and 1971, I moved from the Peace Corps to the legislative side of government as legislative assistant to Senator Edward Brooke. In 1971, I became chief of staff for Walter Fauntroy in the House of Representatives.

As you assess yourself and your dreams, you should consider moving outside your comfort zone. By being willing to do so, you can enhance your career. In addition, it will allow you to connect with people and follow your passions.

Chapter 7
Mentorship: Seeking and Responding to Mentors

Mentorship is another significant facet of advancing your career. Being able to respond to a mentor is a key element of success. That is why you should be open to mentoring, which means being open to someone who wants to support you and give you assistance, someone who believes in you, someone who finds you have potential, and someone who feels that you can add value to their group, organization, or company. Having a mentor is critical to developing your skills.

If you find a person who is in a position that you covet or want to consider, you could seek out him or her as a mentor. Perhaps you can find a way in which you can have discussions or dialogue with that individual.

In many cases, just by being open to mentorship and showing how good and capable you are or showing your willingness to learn, a mentor will find you. People want their organizations and companies to succeed and reach their goals. If you can understand and participate in that, a mentor will find you. Then they will begin to give you coaching, advice, and guidance on how both of you can win. You can win as an employee, and your mentor will win by bringing you onto the team, and thereby allowing the company or organization to excel.

When I was chief of staff for Delegate Walter Fauntroy on Capitol Hill between 1971 and 1973, I learned how the federal government works and how committees work with each other. From my days as a legislative assistant, I learned how legislation is passed. I also learned how member staffs in the Senate and the House work together and how legislation and compromises are made. I was beginning to get a real sense of the value of government. I already knew the executive side, but now I was learning the legislative side.

What I did not know at the time, and what I want you to understand, is that the corporate world values your knowledge of how the federal government works.

I found that the corporate world wanted to know because the federal government impacts business in many ways. For that reason, corporations are looking for persons who have experience and understanding of the federal government.

One day, Harley Daniels, the legislative assistant in Walter Fauntroy's office, approached me and asked if I knew Mr. Charles Weikel of Chesapeake and Potomac Telephone Company, also known as C&P. I had not yet met Mr. Weikel, and I told Harley so. Harley explained to me that Weikel was a Michigan graduate, as was Harley, who would come up to the office and talk about issues that could impact the telephone company. Then he continued, "Well, I have talked with him on a number of occasions.

You may hear from him; I think he might be interested in you." "Interested, how?" I wondered. "Interested in maybe hiring you in the telephone company," Harley replied. I was greatly surprised. I did not know how I would fit into the business world. But both Harley and others told me that companies would be interested in a person who had a sense of government.

Charles Weikel did, in fact, contact me. He invited me to lunch, and we had a great talk. He told me about the possibility of my coming to work at C&P Telephone Company.

At the time, home rule legislation was being considered. Weikel felt that the telephone company would need someone in their organization who could help them if home rule came to the city. If it did, there would be an elected mayor, possibly an elected city council, and there could be an oversight group that would oversee regulatory matters over utilities like telephone, gas, and electric companies.

Weikel talked to me about joining the telephone company to work in public affairs and with the federal government. It was something for me to consider. In such a position, my ten years of federal government experience would be a great asset.

I said yes to the offer, and I moved out of my comfort zone again. There was a possible risk entailed. I was comfortable building a federal career, and it made sense to build on what I had accomplished in the federal government. Now, there was an opportunity for me to get into a challenging, competitive business world using those same skills.

Even though there was some risk, it was exciting to consider how I could use my law degree, my government skills, and my background to work in the competitive regulatory environment of the telephone industry.

I started as a public affairs manager for the Chesapeake and Potomac Telephone Company in 1973, and I spent a total of 21 years there.

C&P consisted of four telephone companies: C&P Telephone of Maryland, Virginia, West Virginia, and the District of Columbia. The four companies of C&P were four of the 22 companies of the old American Telephone and Telegraph (AT&T) system.

As a part of the culture of AT&T and the operating companies, executives were encouraged to be involved in their communities. C&P was no exception. When I was hired there, I too was encouraged to engage myself and volunteer in the community. I worked on The Self-Determination for D.C. Committee, which brought home rule to the District of Columbia. I was very involved in the Greater Washington Board of Trade, which was the Regional Chamber of Commerce. We had community relations teams throughout the company, and we encouraged our employees to volunteer with not-for-profit groups.

I was also involved with the settlement house in southeast Washington called Friendship House. It was one of the settlement house projects that started in Chicago, where community organizations offered services such as daycare, education, and health. It was a very strong community group. I was very active there, and I became the President of the Board of Directors. As a result of my community service, I became well known in the area.

In addition to my involvement with Friendship House, I helped found many of the arts groups in the city. I was President of the Capital Ballet, which was a predominantly African-American Ballet Company. I also helped establish The Cultural Alliance of Greater Washington, which is an almost 40-year old organization that provides support to arts groups across the metropolitan area. C&P's desire for me to be involved in the community fit with my passion for service.

I was the highest-ranking African-American at C&P, the fourth level of management – a division manager. My job was to work with the lawyers on regulatory issues. I was to work with the federal government as home rule was coming to the district and was to begin thinking about how the telephone company might interact with a regulatory commission that could come with the new home rule government.

Chuck Weikel was my boss at the time. He had envisioned that I would join the Greater Washington Board of Trade, so that was one of my first obligations at the company.

The Greater Washington Board of Trade was the regional chamber of commerce and the largest organization of business. I became a member of the board, and I was assigned to work on various committees there. C&P Telephone Company was the largest private employer in the District of Columbia, so we carried great weight in the business community.

The second opportunity that Chuck gave me was to work with the home rule committee, a group called Self-Determination for D.C. Its mission was to draft legislation, which would create a mayor, city council, and a regulatory body that would oversee the utility companies and other local administrative agencies.

I had to listen to my mentor Chuck. I made an effort to get a sense of the business world and to understand what I had to do. I worked hard at it, and I encourage you to work hard at the jobs that you have, understanding that you have been given these opportunities.

In 1974, the home rule bill was passed for the District of Columbia. It created an elected mayor, a 13-member council, which included a chairman; and a regulatory body called the District of Columbia Public Services Commission.

All of the things that Chuck Weikel and the phone company had envisioned happened through this legislation. I had the opportunity to work with the Congress in passing of the home rule bill, which gave the city the right to elect its mayor and its city council. It gave the city a lot more autonomy. It had all the trappings of a local government except for budgetary control, which was retained by Congress. My job at the telephone company was to work hard on those issues.

However, there was a distraction in my mind at the time. I was thinking about my future, and I was very excited about home rule coming to the city. My passion for government, leading, and serving began to raise its head.

We now had a chance to have an elected government with a mayor and city council. Although I had an exciting business career ahead of me, I considered running for office as a candidate for city council.

I thought about running in my ward, Ward 3 of the city, which was a ward in the northwest part of the city. However, there was an appointed councilperson that was going to run for that seat, so I decided to run at large. There were four at-large seats, but the majority party could only hold two seats. I ran for one of the two seats in the Democratic primary.

I knew the risk of following my passion and desire to be a leader in the political realm. There was a possibility that I would have to leave the telephone company after only a year or two of a very promising career. Despite the risk, I made the decision to follow my dream, and I ran for office.

There were nine of us running in the Democratic primary for the two seats. Marion Barry, who I had met before through Walter Fauntroy, was a young civil rights activist. He had great name recognition, and in the end, he came out ahead with several thousand votes. Another civil rights activist, Rev. Douglas Moore, came in second. I lost by a few thousand votes, coming in third out of the nine candidates.

This was one of the times that I did not achieve what I set out to accomplish. However, I ran a good campaign, and I had no regrets about it. I understood politics, and this experience gave me a better sense of what it meant to run for office. I knew about government beforehand, but running for an office was a different story.

The experience of running for office was educational as well as traumatic. The loss was quite a blow to me. I had worked hard and had experienced very few failures previously in life. There had been hardships to endure, but I had not had that many failures. Whenever I did run into an obstacle, I persevered and bounced back.

When I ran for office, I developed a strong political organization. I raised more money than the other eight candidates put together, including Marion Barry. But what I learned was that politics is not just about raising the money. It is also about your message and your name recognition. Though I had a good message, I did not the have necessary name recognition.

I still remember the night of the defeat. My campaign manager said, "You must go out and thank the people for all their support." I was reluctant to do that because I felt so down. How could I go out and thank them? Why did the majority not vote for me? I felt that I was the best candidate.

That night I learned one of the most important lessons of my life; I learned that I was not going to get everything I pursued. I did address the crowd and thanked my volunteers. Like I said earlier, life is about learning how to deal with Plan B when Plan A does not work. I chose to look at the positive; even though I had lost the election, I still had a very promising career at C&P Telephone.

In 1976, when half the council was up for re-election, I considered running again, but Gayle expressed her feelings on the matter very clearly. She said, "If you run, I will divorce you because I think politics is an anathema to the family, and I don't think that is what you should do." I listened to her and did not run.

At C&P Telephone, they still felt that I had promise, and they promoted me to Assistant Vice President in 1976. I was put in charge of public affairs, public relations, and regulatory matters in the company.

I now carried with me the experience of running for office, which gave me an understanding of that process. In addition, I had strong connections to Congress and the political community. Consequently, I was a real asset to the company.

My mentors were critical to my success. When my first mentor at the telephone company, Charles Weikel, was moved to another department head position, I took over his position. Then I reported directly to the Vice President of the telephone company, Ralph Frey.

Ralph had a vision for me that I did not see until later. First of all, he gave me an office next to his. He guided and developed me so that I would be equipped for a very high-level executive position, maybe even replacing him as Vice President and officer of the company.

The population in the District of Columbia was predominantly black. The public school system was over 90 percent black. As the telephone company was the largest private employer in the district, Ralph believed that the head of the telephone company and the leadership should be African-American.

He brought in an African-American lawyer whom he made assistant general counsel and later promoted to general counsel. He brought in another African-American with a financial background to fill the position of assistant controller. After about a year, he moved the controller and put Ed Singletary into that position. Lee Satterfield was the first general counsel, and I was the third manager of color, who was at a high level in regulatory and public affairs.

It was Ralph's vision that one of us would succeed him and become Vice President. I worked diligently, and I listened to him and had faith in him as my mentor.

After I had worked for him for about six or seven years, he retired. Then I was appointed Vice President of C&P

Telephone Company. Consequently, I became the highest-ranking African-American in the company.

It was a great day for me, and I hope that it was a great day for the company as well. It all came about by the vision of one man. The man himself, Ralph Frey, was white. He grew up in Maryland and graduated from the University of Maryland. He had a strong work ethic and believed in people and diversity. He also believed in equal employment opportunity. He brought all those things together and allowed me the opportunity to become an officer of C&P Telephone Company and later Bell Atlantic.

It took me a while to understand Ralph's vision and adapt to the business world. I still had my political connections, but I began to see that this was an opportunity to flourish in the business world. It was an opportunity to excel, and I started to respond and listen to him.

My message to you is to be open to a mentor. I was open to my mentors, Ralph Frey and Chuck Weikel, and that had a large impact on my career. Ralph particularly made an impact on me. He was my guide in helping me learn the business.

I encourage you to listen to your mentor as well. And do not only listen, but also have faith in your mentor, because he or she may see some things in you that you may not see in yourself. Be willing to act and grow with the help that your mentor provides you.

Chapter 8
Partnership

It is very helpful to your career to have partners across the board. That includes partnerships with organizations, family members, and your spouse or close friends. Listen to your partner as you do your mentors.

If you have a strong partnership with a family unit or someone such as an aunt, an uncle, a grandmother, or a grandfather, then keep in mind that what you do impacts those persons. You need to recognize that your actions may impact the actions of others. They have a partnership with you, and they have a dream for you. Hopefully, you have that dream and passion for yourself as well.

In order to succeed, you have to be aggressive. Taking risks, being adventuresome, and working hard is important. You must be single-minded and single focused.

However, as you develop your life and career, you may want to recognize how important it is to compromise. You have to keep in mind that there are other people in life who are important to you. In order to be considerate of them, you may sometimes have to think about compromise as you look for how to manage your life. Think about win-win strategies. Try to find solutions where you win along with your partners, your friends, and your mentors.

You might also want to consider what your priorities are in life. You could be so focused and dedicated to your goal and the plan that you put together that you may lose a sense of what is important in life. What are the values that are important to you, those who care for you, and those who are important to you? Those are the things that you have to keep in mind as you think about your career development and your success.

I was single-minded about running for office. Service and politics were my passions, and I took the chance of running for a position on the city council.

My spouse, Gayle, was very concerned about my running for office because we had four kids, and we were both responsible for their growth and development. Politics, in her mind, only tore us further and further apart. She felt strongly about my not running for office again. As some partners will, she said, in no uncertain terms, that she would divorce me if I ran for office again. Her statement was very direct.

I thought long and hard about my values and priorities, what was important to me and what was important to those around me.

Through my thought process, it became apparent to me that my priority was my family and keeping the family together. I wanted to stay married to Gayle, and I wanted to be with my children and be a part of our family unit.

Growing up in my neighborhood, I saw families that did not always consist of a mother and a father. Several of my good friends were raised by single mothers. These mothers were strong women who cared for their children and provided that strong family unit. There were other friends who were raised by aunts and uncles. To me, that unit was extremely important. Not that my unit was perfect. My mom and dad had their differences, but they stayed together and embraced me and the things that I wanted to do.

My mother was very family oriented. She came from a large family. She had nine sisters and two brothers. Many of her siblings were living while I was growing up, and I got to know them and their children, my cousins, very well.

Every summer, my mother would take me to the small town where I was born, Arkansas City, Kansas, where many of my aunts and uncles lived. We would also visit our relatives in Oklahoma. She took me to these places so that I would get to know my relatives and interact with them.

In addition to all my relatives, I started a family of my own. Gayle and I were married when she was 20 and I was 21, and we had children right away. So family was always an important part of my life.

Since I wanted to stay with Gayle and our boys, I had to figure out how I could balance being a part of the family with my love of service and politics.

I realized that if I were to keep the family together while doing what I loved, there would have to be compromises, and it would have to be on all sides. For example, maybe I could do some things in the community that would be part-time, and Gayle would be supportive, since it would not be full-time political office. I listened to Gayle and her views on politics, and I cared deeply about being a responsible husband and father, helping to raise our four sons.

If you become a parent and you become a partner in a relationship, it is very important to keep that relationship together. It is essential that you take on the responsibility of co-raising your child or children because they are the future of our world.

The relationships you have with your partner and children are binding relationships, and you have an excellent opportunity to make sure that these relationships develop in a constructive fashion. If you are married and if you have children, it is important to balance your career with taking responsibility for your actions towards them.

I have already talked about win-win options and win-win opportunities. I firmly believe that life should be about win-win. Do those things that are good for you and will help others – your partner, your family, or your organization – at the same time.

Obviously, win-lose situations are less ideal, and lose-lose is even worse. I could have chosen a win-lose solution by running for office again in 1976. I believe that I could have won city council if I had run then. Had I run and won, it may have been a win for me career wise. However, it would have been a loss in regards to the family, for Gayle, our boys, and me.

As you strive to balance family and work, you should look for constructive compromises. It is important to avoid trying to blame your partner. Avoid being so headstrong that you say to yourself, “Okay, I’m not going to do this because I value the relationship, but I blame this person because she/he pushes me to make this decision.”

You have to step back and figure out what is important to you. Identify what your priorities and values are, and try to come up with some win-win ideas where the outcome is better for everybody.

Chapter 9
Know and Understand the Culture of Your Business

In order to thrive in a business or an organization, you need to understand its culture. That is true for life in general as well. When I worked for the Peace Corps, and my family and I lived in Nigeria and Uganda, we encountered cultures that were different from what we had experienced in America.

However, you do not have to go all the way to Africa in order to find different cultures. You can experience them right in the United States. I currently live in New Mexico. Here there is a southwestern culture, which is Native American; a Hispanic culture; and influences from the country of Mexico. If you go to parts of western Kansas, you will find a rural culture, a farming culture. I grew up in a segregated culture in Kansas City, Kansas, in an urban setting. You can find a multitude of cultures if you travel around this country.

It is true for organizations as well as businesses that if you are going to succeed and make progress there, you need to understand the culture. All organizations and workplaces have their cultures. You need to identify and learn the culture of where you are. You also need to learn how to manage it because if you move from one place to the next, the culture will be different, and the techniques for thriving in those cultures could differ. The first step, however, is gaining knowledge about it. Living within the culture, making it a part of your life, and becoming consistent or adapting to it is extremely important.

You might have heard about the IBM culture, Big Blue. Everyone at the company wore dark suits, white shirts, and ties, and they had very distinct procedures and processes.

At the old AT&T company, there was also a very distinct culture. Managers were taught to manage with goals and objectives in mind. The mission was to enhance revenues and to keep costs down. They wanted you to be mindful of the bottom line because it was all about generating revenue. These were some of the cultural aspects of the business that you needed to understand.

On the other hand, in the not-for-profit world, the culture is entirely different. The main focus is on service, and there is less emphasis on the bottom line.

Knowing and understanding the culture of the business or the organization you are in, and understanding the systems and the processes, are essential to your survival, your growth, and your success.

When I started at C&P Telephone Company, it was a very different culture from where I had been previously. I had spent ten years in legal and administrative jobs in the federal government. The telephone company was a regulated business.

I was uncertain of whether or not my personality and my passions would fit with my new job because I was interested in people and service. I had a passion for civil rights and trying to change society. Now I was working in a telephone business, and our job was to provide telephone service to our customers. I was not sure this was for me.

After one of my first weeks at the office, I said to Gayle, "I'm not so sure I'm going to survive because it appears that they are more interested in profits than they are in people." That was a problem and a real question mark for me. As I persevered, I got to know the culture and became involved with other managers and the employees. What I found was that yes, they were interested in the bottom line. And yes, you had to understand that by keeping costs down, you could increase that bottom line and produce revenues, which would allow the company to continue being successful in the competitive world. At the same time, this regulated company was involved in the community. It believed in helping those customers that we served. I could see a balance here that attracted me, and I ended up staying 21 years.

In 1993, I had been with C&P Telephone Company for 20 years. I began to reflect on my successful business career but started to question how I could continue to grow. I started thinking that it could be time for a new challenge. It was not to say that my voice had been tuned out or that I was tired of leading the phone company; rather, it was that I had a desire to continue my quest to lead in other areas.

Towards the end of 1993, I received a phone call from the executive search firm Isaacson and Miller. The call came from Arnie Miller, who was a principal in the firm. Arnie invited me to lunch, and he quickly got to the point and asked me if I would be interested in the position as the President of National Public Radio (NPR) headquartered in Washington, D.C. I was deeply flattered and excited, but I knew that such decisions required time and thought, along with sharing the opportunity with Gayle.

Arnie understood, and we agreed that I would get back to him within a short time, so I would not hold up their search process. As I hung up the phone, I realized that this could be the new leadership opportunity that I had been seeking. I discussed the matter with Gayle, and she was very supportive.

After several interviews and taking a long time thinking about it and discussing it, I decided to do it. I was selected by the board of NPR to become its President. In January, 1994, I officially became President of the company.

NPR is a wholly different organization than the one in which I had spent my last 21 years. NPR is a public broadcasting company. It is a not-for-profit company supported by government subsidies and public outreach contributions. However, we still had to maintain some sense of a bottom line so that we could survive and grow.

NPR had a long history of providing excellent programming and informative quality news. As their new President and CEO, I had to learn how to manage this company. It was an opportunity for me to lead and utilize my skills. The downside was that I knew nothing about media. I was not a journalist, and I had never been involved with live programming. However, the opportunity to take my leadership skills and apply them to a less familiar atmosphere was a risk and challenge that I was willing to take.

My first few months were quite rocky because the culture was very different from other cultures I had experienced. NPR was based on a cooperative model. It started in the 50s as educational radio on college campuses. These stations came together as a cooperative and called themselves National Public Radio. NPR included other stations that had licenses from the Federal Communications Commission (FFC) to do educational programming. These like-minded stations came together to become member stations of National Public Radio.

A 17-member Board of Directors governed NPR. At the time of my presidency, there were ten members who were elected by station managers and six at-large members who were appointed by the board. The President and CEO, who was hired by the Board of Directors, was a voting member of the board. The cooperative membership controlled the board and the decisions of the company along with six at-large members.

When I joined the company as the President and CEO in 1994, NPR was doing well. However, it was experiencing some challenges. Speaker Newt Gingrich and some members of the House of Representatives decided to zero out federal funding for public broadcasting. I had the challenge of trying to keep that bottom line healthy.

At the same time, I was learning how the NPR system worked. There were some 600 stations in the NPR system, with stations purchasing the programing produced by NPR. What was unique about the NPR system was the governance/membership model. For example, the same station managers who purchased NPR programs also elected 10 of the 17 board members who had governing power over NPR process and policies; including the hiring and firing of the CEO.

I had to understand how to relate to the board of station managers. Then I had to learn how to relate to the broader group of stations around the country. In addition, I had to understand how to present and develop programs to which our listeners would continue to listen and subscribe. It was challenging.

After about three months, I was unsure if this job was for me. I called the chairman of the board, Carl Matthusen, who was the station manager in Phoenix. Carl had a stake in my success because he was chair of the board, and he was on the committee that selected me as a CEO. I spoke to Carl on the phone, and I told him how I was unsure that I could survive because the culture was so challenging. He came to Washington, and we sat down for about an hour or two. I told him that I was not so sure that the job was a fit. Carl's response was to tell me about the culture of the company. He gave me a history lesson about public broadcasting and about how NPR started. Then he talked to me about the stations and the board.

The conversation took about two or three hours. I began to realize that if I were going to continue as the President and CEO, I would have to have a deeper understanding and acceptance of the culture. I understood that it did not operate like the business that I was in for 21 years, and it certainly did not operate as the federal government. It operated in its own way as a public broadcasting entity.

If I were going to continue working for the company, I would have to understand its processes and methods. I had to accept them and figure out how to work within the culture in order to make it grow and develop.

I stepped back, and I said, "Okay, I'm going to have to compromise a bit. I'm going to have to listen more. I'm going to have to understand this culture and begin to live within this culture and make it work." And that was what I did. I stepped back and spent more time visiting stations. I spent a lot more time talking to station managers. Then I began to put people in place that I trusted. I started developing and managing a strong administrative model at the company. We set goals and objectives, and things began to work.

I had to come back to my basic premise that you have to know and understand the culture and begin to live and work in it to be able to survive, grow, and succeed. I ended up spending almost five years as the President of National Public Radio. When I left, I felt I had done more than a good job. I believe I left the company in much better shape than I had found it.

In order to be successful in an organization and a business, you need to understand the culture. All businesses and organizations have cultures. My very first job was at a jewelry store. That job too required that I understood my responsibilities. There I polished the silver and kept the windows and the counters clean, and so on. The culture there was to serve people in a retail environment.

When I went to work at the telephone company, I had to understand what a regulated utility did in terms of providing telecommunication services. I also needed to understand how it helped and served in the community. National Public Radio was a public broadcasting entity controlled by station managers and operated by station managers. When I came there, I had to figure out how to survive and grow given a cooperative model of business.

My message to you is that you first of all need to recognize that there is a culture in your workplace or organization. Then get to know that culture. Understand it and get a sense of the processes and the procedures that are in place. Once you do that, you will find out whether it fits you or not. If it fits, then you can figure out a way you can manage it to make it work best for you.

Chapter 10
Conclusion

How you can make the system work for you? The first thing you can do is to develop a plan of action. Consider where you would like to be in five to ten years from now. I call it the endgame. By thinking about your endgame, you can determine what it takes to get you there.

If you have begun to discover your passion and assessed who you are, then you are well on your way to finding a career. You might not be sure about the future, but you do need a plan.

Here is an example: You are currently a medical tech and you want to become a physician's assistant or a doctor. Then the first step is figuring out what it will take to get to your endgame. If you want to be a doctor, you will obviously have to go back to school. You will have to complete medical school and a residency. That is the goal.

Start with the endgame, the goal, where you would like to be five to ten years from now. Then work backward; figure out what will it take to get to the endgame and get the results you want.

There is a saying that goes as follows: "If you're not sure where you're going, any road will take you there." If you have a sense of where you would like to be, then the road becomes somewhat clearer. There may be obstacles along the way, but your focus will make it easier. You have a sense of the endgame, and you are headed towards results.

Another key piece to a successful career is what I call principles of living, or rules by which to live. These principles of living have put me in good stead, so I would like to share them with you. I believe they can help you as you develop your career and move forward.

The first principle is to treat people like you would like to be treated. In biblical terms, it is to do unto others as you would have them do unto you. There is a saying that goes as follows: Be careful as you ascend the ladder and be nice to the people who you are dealing with as you ascend the ladder because you may run into those same people when you are on your way down. That is one of the reasons why it is important to treat people like you would like to be treated.

The second principle is always to act with honesty and integrity. Doing so will keep you in good stead. Say to yourself, "Is this honest? Would I be proud of this? Would my mother, father, aunt, or uncle be proud if I say or do this?"

Thirdly, be punctual. Be on time. That sets you apart from others who are developing their career, or maybe even compete with you. When you have a time schedule, and you need to be somewhere, then be punctual. Or if you have a report that is due, then get that task done on time. In addition, be prepared for opportunities. If you know that there is an opportunity, and you know that you have to develop a skill to make sure that you can take advantage of that opportunity, then develop that skill so that you can take advantage of the opportunity.

The fourth principle is to work hard and persevere. It goes without saying. In order to get to where you want to go, in order to get to that endgame, you have to work hard. You have to keep moving forward. You have to pay attention and be focused on all the things needed to reach that endgame, and you have to persevere. Yes, there will be obstacles in the road. Yes, there will be disappointments and failures. But you must keep moving forward and persevere. These principles of living will help you reach your endgame.

When I first came to the National Public Radio, our main audience at National Public Radio at the time was 55 years old or older. So when I set goals and objectives, I realized that if we were going to survive and be competitive in the technological age at that time we had to attract younger listeners.

I also recognized from my telecommunication days that technology was moving fast. People were beginning to use the Internet. There were now many channels and sources where people could find news. Why would they listen to National Public Radio? We had to figure out how we could be competitive. We had to use technology to our advantage.

To meet the challenges above, I did two things. Firstly, I decided to take my chief of engineering and make him chief technology officer. Then I promoted a young man to be the chief engineer. The newly appointed chief technology officer's job was to look at the technologies that were emerging and begin to think how NPR could become a part of those technologies.

One of the things we did was a pilot program with ABC and REAL Networks, where you could see Morning Edition on your computer, and you could hear the voice of Bob Edwards, who was the moderator of Morning Edition, on your computer. That sounds old now, but in '95 and '96, it was cutting edge to bring National Public Radio into the Internet and be competitive as technologies were emerging.

I had to think about how to pay for all of this. The federal government was beginning to talk about cutting our subsidies, although we won that argument. But it still came up every year. Why should the federal government be supporting NPR? In addition, we always felt that our smaller stations did not have the wherewithal to raise the funds; the federal subsidy was very important.

Overall, I felt we needed to increase our fundraising base for National Public Radio. My management team and I created the National Public Radio Foundation. The mission of the Foundation was to attract donors to raise funds to produce quality news and cultural programing for NPR. To this day, money is raised to ensure the long-term viability of NPR.

"No one told me I couldn't" is the mantra by which I have lived. The world is open to opportunity. It has been up to my taking advantage of those opportunities. No one told me I could not achieve. Even though there have been obstacles, particularly as I grew up in a segregated environment, no one told me I could not accomplish what I set out to do.

In the first part of this book, we talked about discovering your passion – discovering the things that you care about – and beginning to act on those things. What is your passion? What makes you excited about life? Discover your passion.

You can do a self-assessment in order to find out who you are, what you do best, what are your positive qualities and strengths. You do need to think about your weaknesses as well, but first and foremost consider your strengths, and think about how you can begin to build on those strengths.

As you discover your passion, you start to connect with people. You cannot move your career forward unless you do so. Almost each step of my career, there was one or several individuals who believed in me and looked out for me. Somebody decided to give me a referral, offer me a job, or give me a call about an opportunity. I began to prepare for those opportunities and take advantage of them.

Discover your passion. Assess who you are, what you can do, and your strengths. Then you can begin to develop your endgame. Once you have done that, then connect with people who can help you to get there. That is when you can achieve success in life.

Success is not to own a fancy automobile or extravagant house, or have a six-figure income. Success concerns how you feel about yourself. Did you reach your goals? Do you feel good about where you are? Do you feel positive about your career? If not, what are you going to do about it? How are you going to make those changes? How are you going to adapt to the changing society and changing world?

I believe you can succeed. It all depends on you and your motivation. It depends on how you make personal assessments, how you develop your endgame, and how you get to where you want to be. It all begins with self.

I have been very fortunate in life. The family unit that I had when I grew up was strong; my mother and father cared about me. I received a good educational foundation. After high school, I built upon that foundation by attending the University of Kansas. There I studied political science and history because I wanted to be a lawyer.

Relatively early in life, I knew that I wished to be a lawyer. That was my self-assessment. I wanted to serve and help people, and I thought that the best way to do that was through the rule of law. Therefore, I went on to Washburn Law School, and that was where I obtained my law degree in 1963. Along the way, I found my life partner, Gayle. So I got a partner, a dream, and an idea of where I wanted to be. In Washington, D.C., I began to set out to accomplish my endgame.

If you follow the principles of living, and if you decide to give self-assessment a try, then I think you too can reach your endgame.

After I had completed my education, I worked in the federal government for ten years. I began in the Justice Department and went on to the Equal Employment Opportunity Commission. Then I joined the United States Peace Corps in Nigeria and Uganda. From there I went to Capitol Hill, the Senate, and the House.

Then I moved into a different realm and spent 21 years in telecommunications where I learned more about how businesses operate. Finally, I started working for the National Public Radio, which was a very exciting opportunity for sharing information and news.

The experience I gleaned from working for the government, private business, not-for-profit organizations, and public broadcasting positioned me well.

Then one day in December 1998, I received a call from Vice-President Gore. He said that he was calling on behalf of President Clinton, who wanted to nominate me as the next United States Ambassador to the Republic of South Africa. I had no idea that I was being considered. I was honored by this call. I turned to Gayle and said, with tears in my eyes, "The President wants to nominate me as the U.S. Ambassador to the Republic of South Africa." She shook her head and said yes. I returned to the phone, and I said, "Mr. Vice-President, I accept." He said, "Congratulations. You'll hear from the State Department."

That was the beginning of another new adventure, one that I had not anticipated – to serve our country as the United States Ambassador to the Republic of South Africa.

That had never been my endgame. My endgame had been to be a lawyer, serve, care for my family, and be responsible.

To be an ambassador and to represent the United States is a high honor to whatever country you have the opportunity to serve. But for me to be the U.S. Ambassador to the Republic of South Africa was a double honor. Not only did I get to be an ambassador, but I also got to be an ambassador to the great country of South Africa.

South Africa had just come through the first democratic elections, where Nelson Mandela was the first democratically elected President in 1994. He served five years.

When I arrived in 1999, Mandela had just stepped down. In their second election, Thabo Mbeki, who had been Mandela's Deputy President, became President. For a year and a half, I had the great honor to serve in this country that was evolving toward a democracy. Similarly, as the United States was coming through our segregated environment, South Africa was coming through Apartheid and dismantling a divisive and segregated society. South Africa was coming through and making great strides. Again, I was honored to be a part of that evolution toward democracy in South Africa from 1999 to 2001.

You too can succeed. You too can reach your endgame and more. You can implement these ideas of discovering your passion, connecting with people, finding your niche, persevering, and reaching for your endgame for success in life. It begins with you; it all begins with self!

Made in the USA
Columbia, SC
13 September 2018